NOTHING more to SAY

NOTHING more to SAY

MAGALY HERIVEAUX

Nothing More to Say

Copyright © 2021 by Magaly Heriveaux. All rights reserved.

No part of this publication may be reproduced, stored in a retrieval system or transmitted in any way by any means, electronic, mechanical, photocopy, recording or otherwise without the prior permission of the author except as provided by USA copyright law.

The opinions expressed by the author are not necessarily those of URLink Print and Media.

1603 Capitol Ave., Suite 310 Cheyenne, Wyoming USA 82001
1-888-980-6523 | admin@urlinkpublishing.com

URLink Print and Media is committed to excellence in the publishing industry.

Book design copyright © 2021 by URLink Print and Media. All rights reserved.

Published in the United States of America

Library of Congress Control Number: 2021903163
ISBN 978-1-64753-699-2 (Paperback)
ISBN 978-1-64753-702-9 (Digital)

09.02.21

DEDICATION

I would like to take this time to dedicate this book to my mother, Bertha Heriveaux, for investing so much of her time in me. Ever since I was young she has always taken a special interest in me and encouraged me in whatever way that she can. She has always believed in my success and has consistently shown her support over the years. As far as I'm concerned, no one can say they have a good mother unless they've had you. I thank God for you!

Likewise, I dedicate this book to my father, Max Heriveaux, who was also equally as supportive of my dreams and aspirations. He always had my best interest at heart, even until the very end in 2003 (R.I.P.).

It is also my intention to dedicate these poems to everyone else so that they feel uplifted and inspired. I hope these poems speak to you in the way that they speak to me. May you be richly blessed!

ACKNOWLEDGEMENT

I would like to thank my Uncle Lionel Heriveaux, Aunt Maryse Heriveaux, Aunt Ghisline Heriveaux-Mucius, and Uncle Mathieu Mucius for always having a positive word to say in anything that I try to do. They are a big source of encouragement and have always shown their support and love throughout the years with their warmth and generosity towards me. The same goes for my cousins Esther Ducrepin., Jean Richard Ducrepin., and Jean Robert C. There are so many family members to mention it would take all day.

I also do not want to forget to mention some of my positive friends like Joleita S., Sandii A., Dawn H., Stephie A., and countless others who always encourage me. Their positive attitude has a great impact on me and my spiritual life. I sincerely appreciate everyone's support.

TABLE OF CONTENTS

Dedication 5
Acknowledgement 7
Introduction 11

I-Dawn

My God is My A-Z 15
Free to Be 16
Negativity Can't Stop My Progress 17
Lead You Forward 18
Don't Ever Stop 19
Rise Up 20
One in the Same 21
I'm a Living Miracle 23
Diamond 24
Indigo Skies 25
Won't You Say? 26
Urban Blues 27

II-Mid-Day

Keep On 31
Fizzle 32
No More 33
Paper Mache 34
I Will Never Stop 35
I Will Live Anyway 36
Never Stop Trying 37
I Used to Be 38
My Walking Shoes 39

Time for Something New 40
What More? 41
Nothing More to Say 42
Little Sister 43
Give It Back 45
Pretty Lady 47
Biscuits 'n' Gravy 49

III-Dusk

Vinegar 53
Not Easy to Shatter 54
I'm Not the One 55
To All the Naysayers 56
Doesn't Matter 57
Not Afraid 58
Anything for Jesus 59
Comatose 60
Behind My Back 61
It's Laughable 62
You Can't Convince Me 63
I Do Not Care 64
Gum Beneath Your Shoe 65
Condition 66
I've Come to Understand 67
What Did You Think? 68
Isn't' It Funny? 69
It's Inconceivable 70
Don't Disrespect Me 71
You Can't Control 72
By Nightfall 73

Epilogue 75
Bibliography 77

INTRODUCTION

Turn every curse sent my way into a blessing. Nehemiah 13:2 NIV

Ouch!

My mother once told me a charming story about how her friend met her husband. The scenario is very ironic because if the couple was not open-minded things would have turned out differently and they would have lost out on a wonderful lifetime blessing.

Josette was riding a bus and waiting for her stop. While she was sitting down some more people go one at one of the busier stops. After everyone stepped in the bus made a sudden movement which caused a gentleman to step on Josette's foot. She was very upset about this and started to argue with the man. He apologized to her several times and continued to speak to her until it was her stop. They kept in contact with each other and eventually got married and stayed married for fifty years.

Isn't it funny what was meant to sour her day turned out to be a lifelong blessing? This is what happens when you staying a very spiritual place with God. Things begin to turn around for you and slowly but surely you will start to see more of God's intervention in your life in bigger and more powerful ways.

Life's difficulties are meant to not only challenge you but grow you as well. In some instances these initial difficulties can turn into very special blessings like it did for Josette. I'm pretty sure she wasn't happy that she said "ouch" at that moment, but I'm even more certain that she didn't think about her foot anymore when she found her wonderful soul mate.

DAWN

My God is My A-Z

My God is my:

Apple in my pie.
Bread in my pudding.
Carrot in my cake.
De in my light.
Egg in my roll.
Fruit in my salad.
Granola in my bar.
Ham in my burger.
Ice in my cream.
Jelly in my donut.
Kernel on the cob.
Latte in my mug.
Meat in my loaf.
Nectar in my rine.
Oxy in my gen.
Peanut in my butter.
Quantum in my theory.
Raisin in my bread.
Sun in my shine.
Tuna in my fish.
Under in my statement
Vanilla in my bean.
Water in my melon.
X in my ray.
Yolk in my eggs.
Zone in my time.

Free To Be

With God I'm free to be how he designed me to be.
He gives me room for creativity.

He always knows just what I need.
He allows me to shine for him endlessly.

With God I'm free to be all he intended me to be.
He never ever tries to stifle me.

I'm free to express myself and be carefree.
He's happy to see me flourish in the way he would like to see.

With God I have this liberty.
He's given us each talents that can help us lead.

We each have something that we can give.
I want to serve him, so that's how I chose to live.

Negativity Can't Stop My Progress

Negativity can't stop my progress if God is with me.
Can't stop my progress if he is the only one who leads.

Oppression is man-made and has no room in glory.
Life is a power struggle. It's the same old story.

Negativity can't stop my progress if my days are ordained.
Don't care for superficial things or for any fame.

I'm not trying to bother anybody or create an awful stench.
I do not care to be in the limelight or warm up the bench.

All I want to do is be a blessing to anyone that I can.
I'll leave it all to Him. He carries the plan.

I'll continue to look to Him in everything I do.
Negativity can't stop my progress 'cause God will see me through.

Lead You Forward

When God tries to lead you forward, negativity will try to pull you back.
There will always be that one person who tries to pull you off track.

It doesn't make a difference; I know my worth in Christ.
I do not need your approval. Jesus has already paid the price.

When God tries to lead you forward, negativity tries to slow you down.
When God blesses you anyway, the word you say is "confound."

That's exactly how some will feel when they wanted the worse for you.
Never let go of his hand and he will show you what to do.

When God tries to lead you forward, expect conflicts to come your way.
These situations come to make you stronger. Don't let your hope be taken away.

There mere fact that you are living means today is not in vain.
He's able to lead you in the calm times and also through the rain.

Don't Ever Stop

Don't ever stop trusting.
Discontinue all the fussin'.

Don't ever stop loving.
Discontinue saying your nothin'.

Don't ever stop caring.
Discontinue greed and start sharin'.

Don't ever stop living.
Discontinue sadness and start givin'.

Don't ever stop seeking.
Discontinue ignorance and start readin'.

Don't ever stop coping
Discontinue self-pity and start hopin'.

Rise Up

Rise up out of bed and pray.
Count your blessings throughout the day.

Tell your loved ones that you care.
Stay clear of greed and learn to share.

Live for love and nothing else.
Avoid crude people, who think of themselves.

Keep your spirits up continue to strive.
Confound others as you continue to thrive.

Stay away from people who can't rebuke you to your face.
Get rid of exploitation. It's all over the place.

Do not be ruled by intimidation.
Say you've had enough.
Start each day with fresh anticipation.

One in The Same

We are all one in the same as God would have it to be.
Some of us have forgotten all about this decree.

As soon as prosperity knocks on the door,
the voice of the Lord we hear no more.

Our titles and positions are all that we see.
Too busy to care. Too *holy* to please.

"You're not my problem," I hear one say.
"Come again another day."

"I need to impress an important man,
 he holds my salary in his hands."

God intended more in the world we see.
He envisioned love and unity.

Stock Markets crash. Gas prices rise.
All that's here are a pack of lies.

Nothing is certain. Nothing' is sure.
No amount of money seems to hold the cure.

Our priorities have become all out of whack.
We strive to be like the upper class.

In Jesus Chris nothing can divide.
No race, no creed, nor mountain high.

For we are all one in the same as God would have it to be.
We were meant to love and live in peace.

Influence and power are as transient as can be.
Bonds and riches will turn to debris.

Luxury homes and trendy cars
still can't compare with shining stars.
God has carefully placed them in the sky above
and tells about his undying love.

We are all one in the same as God would have it to be.
Saved by his grace we are all redeemed.

I'm a Living Miracle

I'm a living miracle no matter what anyone may say.
God continues to work on me each and every day.

Scientist try their best to determine the origin of man.
What they do not realize is that God holds the plan.

He is the author of creation and every human life.
Jesus died for our sins...the utmost sacrifice.

This knowledge gives me value each and every day.
I'm a living miracle no matter what anyone may say.

My mother's womb sheltered me while God designed my being.
All of his wondrous works keeps me believing.

I'm a living sacrifice no matter what anyone may say.
Each day I breathe the breath of life 'cause he rose from the grave.

People savor over gossip, laugh and line up to hear some more.
What should be considered communal bliss has turned rotten to the core.

My existence is quite humbling since he knows everyone by name.
Regardless, God still calls me unique and he remains just the same.

Life and death are a mystery, far beyond the eye can see.
Having Jesus daily keeps me grounded and gives me peace.

I may not be popular or trendy but my God shapes the clay.
God declares me a living miracle no matter what anyone may say!

Diamond

You're a diamond in the rough and are priceless to him.
You're a treasure above all else and are destined to win.

As a diamond in the rough there will be struggles you have to face.
But with God in your life all of those edges will be erased.

You're a diamond in the rough. God is waiting on you.
If you give your life to him, he will see you through.

You're a rare gem who is also very tough.
But he will never set you down because you are a diamond in the rough.

Indigo Skies

The indigo skies are as serene as can be.
They sing to my soul with harmony.

They speak of creation so grand.
It was created by the maker's hand.

The stars glisten their light in the indigo skies.
Their beauty helps to create a contrast so bright.

The velvet night covers the earth with its splendor.
What I would give to see God. What could I render?

I love him so and am in awe or all his might.
I love seeing the stars in plain sight.

He is so great, he's the author of all.
When I look at the skies unto him will I call.

During the night all seems so calm.
The twilight glitters as it waits for dawn.

The indigo skies are filled with mystique.
This beauty is flawless no one else can compete.

My God is majestic in all that he does.
He is the only true Dove.

He is awesome in power and full of might.
That's why he created the indigo skies.

Won't You Say?

Won't you say you love me? Won't you say you care?
I have a purpose for you that's why I've placed you there.

I want to see you flourish. I want to see you grow.
Don't you see I love you? I think you out to know.

Won't you say you love me? Won't you say you see?
I've laid my life for you to create a life of peace.

I will keep my promise. I want to keep my vow.
I've prepared a place for you starting from now.

Won't you say you'll follow? Won't you say you'll try?
My love gets stronger for you as time passes by.

Your love is all I ask for. There are no strings attached.
Although others try to discourage, with me there is no match.

Won't you say you trust me? Won't you follow me today?
When you've learned to trust me, there is always a way.

He is sure to keep his promise each day and every night.
I long to live with Jesus as he prepares my paradise.

Urban Blues

It's time to go home and leave the urban life behind.
I'm tired of the rat race and all the violent crimes.
I'm simply not feelin' this urban life no more.

I'm tired of seeing youth getting hurt and killed all the time.
I want to go home and I want to make you mine.
I'm simply not feelin' this urban life no more.

My Lord why must single mothers suffer and have to make ends meet?
Why are ghettos overcrowded and young boys in the street?
I'm simply not feelin' this urban life no more.

When it's all said and done you love us a whole lot.
You came to save all the "haves and the have nots."
I'm really not feelin' this ghetto fabulous life no more.

The urban blues will soon be a thing of the past.
We will all fly to Glory and be with you at last.
Thank God. We won't have to deal with this urban life no more!

MID-DAY

Keep On

Keep on believing.
Keep on singing.

Keep on trying.
Keep on striving.

Keep on hoping.
Keep on coping.

Keep on dreaming.
Keep on leaning.

Keep on rising.
Keep on climbing.

Keep on learning.
Keep on yearning.

Keep on sharing.
Keep on caring.

Whatever it is that you can keep on doing,
Keep it up until it gets you moving.

Fizzle

Has life lost its' fizzle?
Do you long for something more?

Do not go too far.
Jesus is already at the door.

Do you feel bewildered and wonder what to do?
Take a moment to pause so he can see you through.

Has every option failed you? Have you run out of ideas?
He will guide you through your challenges and wipe away all tears.

Do people willfully abuse you?
Has hatred reared its' ugly head?

Do not let life lose its' fizzle.
Why not give Jesus a try instead?

No More

No more to nightfall.
No more to sorrow.

No more to loneliness.
No more to grey tomorrow.

No more to suffering.
No more to cruelty.

No More to superficiality.
No More to negativity.

No more deception.
No more oppression.

No more heartache.
No more depression.

No more wondering.
No more guessing.

No more worrying.
No more stressing.

Finally, no more of anything that was meant to destroy me.
I shake them all off because Jesus made me free.

Paper Mache

I acknowledge my life is like paper mache.
He upholds me with his hand each and every day.

He always gives me what I need.
He's impartial to all gender, class, race, and creed.

Like paper mache is what I would be,
if I didn't pray to him and let His spirit lead.

We're all made from dust. Life is as fragile as can be.
Our existence is a wonder. We're made so intricately.

Although like paper mache we are deeply rooted in Christ.
His love is above human comprehension. He's made the sacrifice.

We're here for just awhile, so try to do good.
Let us live life in the way we should.

I Will Never Stop

As long as I am breathing, I will never stop.
As long as you have hope your faith will rise you to the top.

God's love is unconditional. He wants us by His side.
You can tell him anything. In him you can confide.

I will never stop living to please somebody else.
God has given me purpose and talents. I will not keep them to myself.

Don't waste your time to try to stop me. My days have been ordained.
He'll make a way out of no way. This promise I will claim.

I will never stop being thankful for everything he has done.
There's no force that can stop his will. Praises to the Father, Spirit and Son.

He'll always have the last say.
Not intimidated by negative tactics that try to get in my way.

I'll never stop believing in brighter days regardless, of who believes in me or not.
God is still really in control, just in case you forgot.

I'll never stop claiming what God has promised me.
A life filled with Joy, love and his perfect peace.

I Will Live Anyway

You do not want to see me happy unless I belong to you.
I will live anyway and pray for my dreams to come true.

You want to keep me close and dictate what I should do.
I will live anyway and wait for God to see me through.

I will not stop longing for the life that God wants for me.
It's not in my nature to embrace negativity.

You'd like to control me and make me function on your terms.
I will live anyway despite discouraging words.

To each he gives a talent that can be used to share his name.
Regardless of what you try. I will live just the same.

You can't seem to grasp this concept and continue to try to hinder me.
Everything happens when it's supposed to. He's the giver of liberty.

Despite how you see me, I already know God's point of view.
Regardless the approval of many or just a small hand few.

Never Stop Trying

Never Stop Trying. God believes in you.
Never stop trying. Trust him in all you do.

Never stop trying. Give him your mind, heart and soul.
Never stop trying. Forget everything you've been told.

Never stop trying. Keep doing your best.
Never stop trying. In him you'll find a sweet rest.

Never stop trying. Hold fast to the ones who care.
Never stop trying. Ignore those who make things hard to bear.

Never stop trying. Give us a new outlook.
Never stop trying. Keep our hope on you as we should.

Never stop trying. Faith and honor belongs to Christ.
Never stop trying. He gave his very life.

Never stop trying. Some will try to get in the way.
Never stop trying. Look to him today.

I Used To Be

I used to be led by fear and worry. It was never a peaceful time.
I didn't know at that moment that with Jesus it would all be fine.

I used to be full of anxiety and also full of doubt.
Then I decided to spend more time with Jesus and found out what faith was about.

Faith was a word I always heard of but never fully understood.
Now that I finally have it, I'm able to live life like I should.

I used to be full of questions, but I've learned to let them go.
It's so much easier to let him guide our lives since he always knows.

I used to sometimes wonder how life would be like for me.
I've learned persistent faith will give me consistent peace.

My Walking Shoes

My walking shoes have served me well, is what I would like to say to Christ.
When I go to Heaven, I will tell all how quickly they made time fly.

They've carried me through good times and carried me through pain.
They've carried me in sunshine. They've carried me in rain.

My walking shoes have served me well but it's time for another chapter.
My God will be with me every single day here and forever after.

My walk with God everyday has helped me to reach others.
We are all responsible to help our sisters and our brothers.

My walking shoes have served me well. That is what I will always claim.
With Jesus by my side each day is never the same.

My shoes have carried me through life's challenges and its rewards.
I will exchange my walking shoes for wings once Jesus opens Heaven's doors.

Time for Something New

Time for something new.
My heart longs for more.

Time for something new.
I do not want loneliness anymore.

Time for something new.
What should I do?

Time for something new.
I'll pray to God to see me through.

Time for something new.
Keep pressing on.

Time for something new.
Keep singing his song.

What More?

Opening your eyes.
Gazing at the skies.

What more is there to life than this?
Talking with love ones for hours.

Smelling the sweetly scented flowers.
What more is there to life than this?

Living to help others.
Learning to love one another.

What more is there to life than this?
Being embraced with a warm hug.

Lying in a cozy bed and feeling snug.
What more is there to life than this?

Appreciating the little things.
Looking for the good that life can bring.
There really isn't more to life than this.

Nothing More To Say

There is nothing more to say. I stand on God alone.
He's my constant inspiration. He's the best friend I've ever known.

He's been with me through the tough times and has picked me up.
When you feel bewildered, ask for strength. He will give you enough.

There's nothing more to say. We need to accept the good and the bad.
When you've mastered this concept you will be very glad.

Just do your very best to live your life each day.
There's no need to get philosophical. Be humble with what you say.

There's nothing more to say, except keep pressing on.
Don't allow yourselves to grow cynical, please hold on to your song.

Life is beyond comprehension and renders you speechless anyway.
It's for this very reason there is nothing more to say.

Little Sister

Little sister, where have you been?
Did you remember who you were before you stepped in?

Did the harshness of the world pull you off your course?
Did you decide that you love yourself without any remorse?

If you do not say what you feel deep inside,
People definitely tell you what to decide.

They will decide if you are deserving enough to have your heart's desire.
That is why *you* must always aspire.

Aspire for greatness in every little deed.
Care for yourself and others no matter how things seem.

Do not let the snags and snares of disappointments keep you bound,
Even in these moments hope can be found.

Kick the dirt from under your feet.
Put your shoulders back and declare liberty.

Liberty to be everything that you are.
Liberty to see the sunrise in the morning and the night time see the stars.

Let your inner core continue to strengthen every day.
Let your pride, self-esteem, and love uphold you in every step you take.

Even until your dying breath,
Never stop believing that you are the best.

Not compared to anyone else,
But simply a wiser version of yourself.

Little sister with all that's been said and done,
If you still value life you've already won.

Your inner zeal cannot be quenched unless you say so.
Illuminate Beauty from within until the outside glows.

I hope these words have encouraged your soul.
May you hold them dear until you grow old.

Self-love is timeless soon you'll see,
everything in life is more than what it seems.

Give It Back

When the label of mediocrity has been imposed on you, give it back!
When the world tries to jeer at you, give it back!

Do not stand to be something that you're not.
Do not accept degradation as your lot.

You are so much more than you think you are.
Push to the limits a vision is never too far.

As any man or woman knows what their worth should be,
They should embrace themselves daily and walk in peace.

Confidence cannot be found in a jar,
Nor can it be worn. We must raise the bar.

When others try to downgrade you,
Give it back and say," I will not look down because you told me to."

I choose not to live inside of a clam and
I dare to dream with everything that I am.

So, with your head held up high and arms open wide,
Kick cynicism and negativity to the side.

Give this back to those who want to give this to you.
You deserve better no matter what you've been through.

Don't ever forget we've been made deep inside in the womb.
Give it back you're alive. You don't belong in a tomb.

Be the hope for the future and let them all see,
Anything can be theirs if they're willing to achieve.

So, give it back so there's room for love, joy, and peace.
Free from all labels and free to be all you were meant to be.

Pretty Lady

Hey pretty lady, they stop and stare.
Pretty lady, they want a share.

They try to cut you down with their words
And tell you all kinds of insults you've never heard.

You are full of life and unique as can be.
You are priceless and meant to be Queen.

God meant this for every wife, sister, daughter, and mother,
And believes each woman is unlike no other.

You were meant to nurture this earth,
And at the same time, exude strength from your birth.

So, why do you suffer so needlessly?
Pack your burdens up and send them out to sea.

Put your head up high no matter what.
You are regal, even if they forgot.

You are full, flourishing, and free.
You are priceless, and deserve a little dignity.

Even if you have been wilted inside,
In time, courage you will find.

So, make the best out of every day,
No matter what those critics may say.

You give to life what you want to come back to you.
Keep on trying until all of your dreams come true.

Remember not to sell yourself short,
Even when things get twisted, and stories contort.

Pretty lady, stand up for who you are.
You are full of substance or they wouldn't try so hard.

You have more to give than you can possibly conceive.
Just take a moment to declare...I believe!

Biscuits 'n' Gravy

You're like biscuits 'n' gravy I want to have you all the time.
I pray out loud or meditate in my mind.

I look for what today can bring;
Look to the skies and begin to sing.

Like flapjacks and that buttery batter;
I'm flipped over until nothing else matters.

Each moment is destined to be
Full of hope and vitality.

You can never stop loving me,
Whether I'm a pauper or a Queen.

And I never stop believing
Even when I'm not seeing.

New hope is found and I know I'm not dreaming.
With new confidence I will speak with feeling.

Orange marmalade awakens your senses.
Sharing love leads to open fences.

Last but not least I will never boast
Move on to joy and bring the toast!

DUSK

Vinegar

Some people's words are like vinegar so why should I hear?
Don't you know my Jesus is always near?

My God sees my value even when some don't.
God forbid I say something kind. I might rock the boat.

Some people's words are like vinegar, pungent and sharp.
Thankfully, Jesus is always in my heart.

No matter what I do or say it's never quite enough.
Since everyone is made from clay anyway why all of the fuss?

We are here but for a moment when it's all said and done.
It's so great to know God send his only Son.

It's so good to know that His love is the same.
He thinks that we are priceless that is why he came.

Some people's words are like vinegar but you know not what you say.
They keep rambling sarcasm and might not even last the day!

Every morning that we wake up is only by grace.
This is not by our power or anyone's eccentric face.

I'm thankful for His love and know that He is true.
He will walk with me today and make me feel brand new.

What can compare to this type of interchange?
Surely not words of vinegar but his love will always remain.

Not Easy To Shatter

I'm not easy to shatter because God has taught me to be
Strong in him regardless of life's cruelties.

Losing loved ones, betrayals and so much more.
I'm not easy to shatter because God is at my door.

Been through tears and frustrations that can't even be verbalized.
Tired of blatant disregard for any efforts to be realized.

So much twists and turns in life that try to keep me still.
Thankfully, I know that the cross was on that hill.

I'm not easy to shatter and I'll keep reaching to Him every single day.
I'm so glad I've made this discovery. He will keep finding a way.

Regardless of life's challenges I know he is my guide.
I'll continue to claim his promises and ask Him to be by my side.

I've learned to reject the things that attempt to make me fight.
He will address any wrongs that have been done in my life.

I've learned to look to him more and more regardless of what comes my way.
He's my source and my inspiration my rock and my stay.

I'm grateful for what he has taught me and what he continues to teach me every day.
I've acknowledged that life with Him is the only way.

I'm not easy to shatter, not because of anything that I do.
I'm not easy to shatter because I trust him through and through.

I'm Not The One

I'm not the one, no matter how hard you try.
God has ordained my days and has a purpose for my life.

Try as you may to knock me off my course,
God will prevail without using any force.

I'm not the one that you can take and toss to and fro'.
Look, I'm simply not the one because God says so.

He knows every number of hairs on my head.
He knew me before I was born. This is why I trust in him instead.

I'm not tying to offend anybody or come across like I'm proud.
I'm simply not the one that has to follow the crowd.

My focus is on Jesus and not on any clique.
He says we all have value and have been carefully hand-picked.

Just simply trying to serve him and live a humble life.
No time for negativity, foolishness or strife.

Now that I've claimed Jesus, God's precious Son,
I can sincerely and happily say, "I'm simply not the one."

To All The Naysayers

To all the naysayers and everyone who disbelieves.
Have you ever tried Jesus? Don't you know he'll never leave?

He's my reason for living, my purpose, my friend.
He will see you through 'till the very end.

To all the naysayers and the one's filled with doubt.
Don't you now God will help you out?

There's no sense in borrowing worry ahead of time.
We should always keep our focus on helping mankind.

Life is full of hurdles. We should all be aware.
Despite of circumstances, we shouldn't act like we don't care.

Skeptics are contagious with no good fruit to bear.
Simply try your best to ignore them and move on from there.

Life was meant to be something that encourages us to care.
It's not supposed to be an experience that would bring wear and tear.

Some people would feel better if they see the good.
Negativity makes it tough to see things the way you should.

So, to all the naysayers I bid you all some peace.
Trust in Jesus to feel complete.

Doesn't Matter

It doesn't matter what people say, do, or try.
You are the apple of God's eye.

It's so nice to know that he cares for you and me.
He will walk with me always from now until eternity.

There will be some who keep us from speaking his name.
His presence and his purpose will always remain.

He was there from the beginning and will be through the end of time.
We will never stop speaking about him because he's yours and mine.

It really doesn't matter what others try to do.
I'm grounded in Christ Jesus his light will come shining through.

Some people need to feel like they have the upper hand.
All the while not knowing he's at the disposal of any man.

He says I am his treasure, his priceless gem and stone.
He already claimed me as his own.

Not Afraid

I'm not afraid of tomorrow; I've tried that route before.
Living life in fear only brought trouble to my heart's door.

Not afraid of tomorrow. What a waste of time.
Why borrow anxiety ahead of time.

You can't go in the future and line up everything in a row.
Nor can you go to yesterday and adjust everything in the way you say so.

Why lose nights of precious sleep for things that are not in your hands?
Try instead to focus on this day that God has planned.

Good bye fear and sadness leave and do not say a thing.
I'm afraid you're too expensive. You'll cost me everything.

I've learned that life without you makes things much easier to bear.
This is the type of news that I want to share.

I'm not afraid of tomorrow, because fear doesn't have any friends.
If you stay in perfect peace, you'll be better off in the end.

Finally free from your clutches that had a mental hold of me.
I owe it all to Jesus, my friend who gives me serenity.

Anything for Jesus

Some people will do anything for success because that's what comes first.
They are driven by a title that cannot quench their thirst.

Power consumes them every day and night.
Willing to do or say anything to win that fight.

Anything for success no matter the price.
If it means stepping on others then it's their right.

Exploitation, degradation, defamation to name just the few.
These are simply some tidbits of what some are willing to do.

Success in its self is not bad thing, you see.
It's how you go about it that makes the experience unique.

God-given success can bless others in need.
He can use you if you let him to plant a seed.

Abuse of power is not equated to success.
It is simply oppression at best.

Once he blesses nothing can stand in the way.
Dissention and all cruelty need to go away.

Anything for success, this not the case.
Pursuing your dreams without God would be the biggest mistake.

Comatose

I'm not supposed to have any feelings. I'm not supposed to bloom like a rose.
Negativity wants me to stay still and be comatose.

I'm not supposed to make any effort to improve my circumstance.
I'm supposed to aimlessly float around and leave everything to chance.

It would be so much easier if we did everything we were told.
If we floated around like a leaf and allowed ourselves to grow cold.

This was never God's intention for us to be placed on a shelf;
Nor does He desire for us to remain flaccid and remain to ourselves.

When we allow ourselves to be comatose it doesn't do us any good.
We are not able to use our talents in the way that we should.

We will never be able to share our gifts to others who are true and dear.
God doesn't want us to stay in this state. He wants us to move in full gear.

Behind My Back

Behind my back is where they belong.
All of the cynics who try to steal my song.

I do not have the time to fight hypocrisy.
I have my vision set on higher sights you see.

I can't dwell on things that don't bring good fruit.
I want to make every effort to thank Him and move on to useful pursuits.

I want to stay focused on whatever is good.
Ignore pessimism as I should.

Behind my back is where they need to stay.
Tearing down friendships all throughout the day.

I'll never stop praying for God's insightful spirit.
I will prosper as long as God is in it.

It's Laughable

It's laughable how some people forget.
Nothing last forever so live peacefully with no regrets.

Some will do all they can to discourage you.
How soon they forget that they are human too.

It's laughable at what people place their importance on.
You wake up today and tomorrow you are gone.

Life is such an unpredictable thing.
You just never know what tomorrow may bring.

With all this in mind why is there so much effort to tear others down?
Jesus is the most consistent source that can ever be found.

When it's all said and done not everyone's priorities are the same.
It's truly laughable. That's why I'm glad I know his name.

You Can't Convince Me

You can't convince me no matter how hard life may try.
Negativity simply wants to convince me I'm not worth the sacrifice.

Thank goodness I do not believe in obstacles but believe in God instead.
I can count on him for big things and even for daily bread.

You can't convince me that my life is in vain.
Regardless of what you try, God will love me just the same.

We were meant to help others, that's what God has decreed.
I will keep striving because I still believe.

You can't convince me that there is nothing good for me.
I've already found this answer. Jesus Christ is the key.

He's already told me that my days are ordained.
That's why you can't convince me negativity will remain.

I Do Not Care

I do not care how hard you try.
I choose life. I will not die.

As long as we are here, we should keep praising His name.
He is my love and I know He feels the same.

I do not care how much others have or about their place in society.
The thing that's most important is how people treat me.

Being a loving person and making God first.
These attributes are priceless and are the things we should thirst.

It doesn't matter what bad things we've been told.
We cannot be replaced and are more precious than gold.

Do not buy into the superficial buzz.
God adores us all and will always show his love.

Gum Beneath Your Shoe

Soon all of your problems will be like gum beneath your shoe.
Just scrap it off and keep walking. It's the only thing to do.

You can't control other people's actions or what they think.
Will you reach out to God for hope or let your heart sink?

It may not always be easy dealing with certain things that come up.
You have to reach a point where you say you've had enough.

Soon all of your problems will be like a piece of gum beneath your shoe.
You shake it off and keep going the distance until things look new.

Old stale gum doesn't keep someone from walking, no matter how annoying it may be.
Just scrap it off and look to God. Trust and wait on him to lead.

Condition

This world wants to condition us to believe,
We have to be like everyone else in order to succeed.

The world wants to condition us by ingraining in our minds
That we aren't really anything. We aren't one-of-a kind.

The world wants to condition us by shredding our self-esteem
That's what some will do to live out their dreams.

The world wants to condition us by breaking us down.
Regardless of gender, race, creed or ethnicity. By any means it can be found.

Some people have a tendency to think of themselves first.
They do not realize without God things will grow worse.

Do not allow anyone to condition you unless it's God alone.
He always has the best intentions and will be the best source you've ever known.

Do not allow anyone to condition you regardless of whom it is.
There is no amount of money or title that will keep you from being his.

I've Come To Understand

I've come to understand not everyone is the same.
Some will do anything just to make a name.

I never understood the depths that some will go.
Oppression is a way of life just to stay afloat.

I've come to understand a cynical heart has no limit.
There's not sense in finding logic if God isn't in it.

Bitterness is draining, apathy has no remorse.
Who can stand against cruelty? Hence, the human condition without God as the source.

I've come to understand what life would be like without Christ.
It would be very unfulfilling and lack meaning. It would bring about strife.

This is why I'm so glad I've learned and continue to learn each day.
I've come to understand that Jesus is my stay.

What Did You Think?

What did you think would happen? That I would curl up and die?
Did you think that I would stop praying or I would throw up my arms and cry?

God has taught me to trust Him when things are good or unclear.
I've gained increasing confidence in God year after year.

He gives me the strength to try again.
I still make an effort even if I do not always know how or when.

I know that I am worthy...worthy because he knows my name.
We are the very reason why he left Heaven and came.

His promises should encourage even if we do not see them take place.
His presence and words uplift us daily, while we are in this rat race.

So, what did you think would happen? Did you think that I'd stop hoping for what's good?
After Jesus left Heaven and did everything that He could?

I know I have an anchor even if life tries to throw lemons my way.
I will brush myself off in the name of Jesus and pray to him each day.

Isn'T' It Funny?

Isn't' it funny how life can be?
Today you're sought after. Tomorrow you're just a memory.

People spend endless time trying to make their point.
They forget God sees through them even down to their joints.

Isn't' it funny how vengeance can be?
It starts out real small and then it spreads like a disease.

Some use their power to take advantage of others circumstance.
These people do not realize with God they won't stand a chance.

Isn't' it funny what some people need to feel good?
They get a rush by controlling others as they feel they should.

There's more to life then the things we're taught to have.
Fellowship, kindness to counter the bad.

We need to refocus our minds, hearts and soul to Christ.
All of our cares and concerns will slowly subside.

It's Inconceivable

It's inconceivable what goes on in some people's mind.
When you open their hearts cobwebs are all you find.

It's inconceivable what goes in this world.
Thankfully God can intervene with just one word.

We go about our duties every day.
We have no clue sometimes what will come our way.

Yet and still some try to minimize your worth.
They forget God ordained your days before your birth.

It's inconceivable how far some will go.
They'll spend half a lifetime proving how much they know.

What a paradigm shift to concentrate on Christ.
He will take all concerns and make them right.

He will take your heart and provide healing you never knew.
He'll hold you daily and make you feel brand new.

Don't Disrespect Me

We can agree to disagree but don't disrespect me.
We can debate world views or the latest currency but don't disrespect me.

I understand we are all unique and realize that we will not always agree.
So, please embrace this concept and please don't disrespect me.

We are all one in Christ and have great seeds within.
He's the giver of all life, and rules the seas and the winds.

He's ordained my days in advance and loves everyone just the same.
He shows no favoritism and gives all a chance. So, just call on his name.

If you chose to reach out to Christ, remember it's for all he paid the price.
So, there is really no excuse to not have unity in Christ.

You Can't Control

You can't control what other people do.
You can only control what you do.

You' can't control what other people say.
You can only control how you conduct your day.

If you keep your focus on what's wrong then you'll never make any effort to try.
Don't spend time asking useless questions like "How come?" or "Why?'

You can't control who chooses to dislike you no matter how nice you try to be.
You can only do your best to live your life in peace.

By Nightfall

When your day seems weary and you've run out of words to say,
Remember to let your cares go by nightfall and look forward to another day.

When you become tired and wish for something new,
Release them all by nightfall. It's the easiest thing to do.

When you become confused and life starts to make no sense.
Let them go by nightfall. Don't nurture these thoughts in bed.

Look to God each morning and make him your priority.
You need something to encourage you so you can help others see.

If you should forget all of the good he has done throughout the day,
Remember to count your blessings by nightfall. Give him thanks when you pray.

EPILOGUE

The Lord delights in those who fear him, who put their hope in his unfailing love. Psalms 147:11 NIV

Keep it Lit

There was a young couple who decided to take a walk through the woods. While they were walking they got lost and it started to get dark. Fortunately, this couple had candles so they can see where they were even though they didn't know where they were going.

While they were walking it started to become very windy. At this point, should the husband say to his wife, "Well, honey. It looks pretty bad. I guess we should blow out our candles and just stand here." What is the likelihood of a man actually saying this to his wife in this situation? Do you really think this is what he said to her in this scenario? I don't think so.

I'm sure his wife would be inclined to think that they should keep on walking and keep their candle lit. Imagine while they were walking it started to get windy, cold rain began to pour down and loud bursts of thunder and lightning bedazzled the dark sky. You could only imagine their horror and unsettling predicament.

It would be pretty ridiculous for the husband to suggest that the elements have gotten worse and they should definitely blow out their own candles. It's at that very crucial moment that they need their candles the most to help them out of their forest.

That's what hope in God is like. We have to always make sure that we keep our candle lit. We can blow out our own candle by focusing on the wrong things. Likewise, others including family members and friends can also blow out your candles by continually speaking words of discouragement and defeat to you. When it's strangers or acquaintances who speak defeat it is easier to brush off. If family members or friends engage in this type of talk, it becomes more challenging to keep it lit. Negative self-talk is even more detrimental to us than anything else. That's why we need to always stay focused on speaking words of life to keep our candle lit.

We can only sense how dismal the situation would be if that young couple blew their own candles out or allowed the wind to blow it out. Then what? That's how strong our hope has to be. The worse our situation is the more we have to fight to hold on to our hope. The second we give up hope, the more our problems will become magnified.

Hope cannot be just mere words; it has to be an action that is applied. That is why action verbs are called just that. They require action. Make sure all of your words and action always causes you to keep your candle lit.

BIBLIOGRAPHY

Born and raised as a Christian in Brooklyn, New York to very loving parents, who stayed together for over 40 years. Also, I had a spiritually relentless grandmother who lived until age of 96. Resided in the state of Michigan from 1989-1995 and completed an undergraduate and graduate degree in Psychology. Worked in the Social Service field in New York over the next few years and traveled abroad to Mexico, Barbados, Jamaica and Germany. Afterwards, complete another graduate degree in 2005, while residing in New York State.

Currently single, and enjoys visiting friends, family, cooking, writing, and going to concerts. Loves to encourage and make people laugh. Derives a lot of strength from reading and believing Psalms 139.

www.ingramcontent.com/pod-product-compliance
Ingram Content Group UK Ltd.
Pitfield, Milton Keynes, MK11 3LW, UK
UKHW022220230426
12048UKWH00016BA/960